New book releases are free the first 48 hours. Every month, there is a free download on Kindle. To know of new releases and dates for free downloads, please subscribe at

www.TessaCason.com

Tessa Cason
5694 Mission Ctr. Rd. #602-213
San Diego, CA. 92108
www.TessaCason.com
Tessa@TessaCason.com

LEGAL NOTICE AND DISCLAIMER:

From author and publisher: The information in this book is not intended to diagnose or treat any particular disease and/or condition. Nothing contained herein is meant to replace qualified medical or psychological advice and/or services. The author and publisher do not assume responsibility for how the reader chooses to apply the techniques herein. Use of the information is at the reader's discretion and discernment. The author and publisher specifically disclaim any and all liability arising directly or indirectly from the use or application contained in this book.

Nothing contained in this book is to be considered medical advice for any specific situation. This information is not intended as a substitute for the advice or medical care of a Physician prior to taking any personal action with respect to the information contained in this book. This book and all of its contents are intended for educational and informational purpose only. The information in this book is believed to be reliable, but is presented without guaranty or warranty.

By reading further, you agree to release the author and publisher from any damages or injury associated with your use of the material in this book.

80 EFT Tapping Statements™ for Addictions

Includes a Bonus of 60 Extra Statements

Tessa Cason, MA

My EFT Tapping Story

I established a life coaching practice in 1996 when life coaching was in its infancy. After several years, I realized that desire, exploration, and awareness did not equate to change and transformation for my clients.

Exploring the underlying cause of their pain, knowing their motivation to change, and defining who they wanted to become, did not create the changes in their lives they desired.

My livelihood was depended on the success of my clients. I realized I needed a tool or technique or method to aid my clients in their quest for change.

At the time, I knew that everything in our lives, all of our thoughts and feelings, choices and decisions, habits and experiences, actions and reactions were the result of our beliefs.

I knew that the beliefs were "stored" in our subconscious mind.

I knew that to transform and change our lives, we needed to heal the underlying unhealthy, dysfunctional beliefs on the subconscious level. I needed a tool, technique, or method to eliminate and heal the beliefs stored in the subconscious mind.

I visited a friend who managed a bookstore and told her of my dilemma, that I needed something to help my clients truly change and transform their lives. She reached for a book on the counter, near the register. "People have been raving about this book on EFT, Emotional Freedom Technique. Try it and see if it can help your clients."

In the 1990s, the internet was not an everyday part of our lives. Popular books sold more by word of mouth than any other means. Managing a bookstore, my friend knew what worked and what did not work. I trusted my friend, so I purchased the book.

As I read the book and discovered that EFT was tapping our head, I was unsure if this was the technique that would help my clients. I had some adventurous and forgiving clients whom I taught how to tap. When **every single client** returned for their next appointment and shared how different their lives had been that week because of tapping, I took notice! I was intrigued.

I learned that the first statement we needed to tap was: "It's not okay or safe for my life to change."

I learned that when a tapping statement did not clear, it meant there were other dysfunctional beliefs preventing the statement from clearing. When a statement didn't clear, I turned the statement into a question.

I learned that for EFT Tapping to work, we needed to find the cause of an issue.

I learned that clearing an emotional memory was different from clearing dysfunctional beliefs.

I learned that tapping one side of the body was more effective that tapping both sides simultaneously.

Clients started asking for tapping homework. I wrote out statements for them to tap. Soon, I had a library of tapping statements on different emotional issues.

I have been an EFT Practitioner since 2000. Working with hundreds of clients, one-on-one, I learned how to successfully utilize EFT so my clients could grow and transform their lives.

TABLE OF CONTENTS

Chapter 1
Intro

* When our lives feel hopeless
* When we feel empty inside
* When we feel hollow and shallow
* When we feel as if we are squandering our lives away
* When we feel our lives have no purpose
* When we feel life itself has no purpose
* When we feel we are not fulfilling our destiny
* When we feel we have no destiny
* When we feel our actions are useless
* When we feel we don't have the talents and abilities to be successful

Rather than feel pain, we reach for something and/or someone outside ourselves to numb the pain of our shame, guilt, apathy, fear, and/or anger. Continuing to reach for the substance, day after day after day becomes an addiction.

Addictions might be about:

* Anger. Anger that we do not believe we have the tools, talents, skills, intelligence, abilities, capabilities, and/or wisdom to be loved, successful, prosperous, powerful, accepted, joyful, peaceful, happy, and/or cherished. Anger that we do not know how to learn or acquire these skills.

* Punishment. We are punishing ourselves for lacking the emotional courage to deal with life.

* Hiding. Addictions may be a way of hiding from ourselves and others.

* An illusion of "depth" and "substance." The addictive high provides an illusion of power and depth for the addict that feels shallow, insignificant, and unworthy.

* An attempt to feel and experience happiness and peace. The addictive high deadens the lower energies of grief, apathy, guilt, and shame, allowing the addict to experience the higher altitudes of love, peace, and joy.

* An addiction to pain, fear, and/or anger. The future looks hopeless and futile. Addicts will do something now that will keep them in the past, so they don't have to deal with their fear of the future. Fear, anger, resentment, and guilt keep us tied to the past.

All fear might actually be anger...anger that we do not have the tools to heal the past. Anger is the past; fear is the future. Fear is anger that we failed at something in the past and believe we will fail again in the future.

There is something that will heal our addictions. It's called EFT Tapping, Emotional Freedom Technique.

Alcohol or drugs do not have the power to create a 'high' at all. The actual effect of drugs is merely to suppress the lower energy fields, thereby allowing the user to exclusively experience the high ones. Rarely does the average person get to experience love without fear, or pure joy, much less ecstasy. But these higher states are so powerful that once they have been experienced, they are never forgotten and therefore, are sought ever after. It is to this experience of higher states that people become addicted.

David Hawkins

Chapter 2
Derrick's Story

Derrick's parents had a shotgun wedding when they were seniors in high school. He was born two months after his parents graduated from high school. Derrick is an only child and is very close to his mom. She was a very loving, gentle woman, and Derrick was an only child.

Derrick's father works as a mechanic. Throughout Derrick's childhood, his dad shifts from one job to another. He was always fired for the same reason: drunk on the job. His dad is a raging alcoholic. Derrick swore he would never be like his dad.

During Derrick's senior year in high school, his mom was diagnosed with breast cancer and was gone within six months. Derrick was devastated.

The day his dad and Derrick return home from the funeral, his dad tells Derrick that he is on his own as soon as he graduates from high school. He wants him out of the house and doesn't care if he ever returns. His dad tells Derrick he is a loser. Always had been and always would be. His mom was too soft on him. He would never be a man, strong and proud.

On graduation day, Derrick enlists in the army. After boot camp, he is sent to the war in Vietnam. Since no one was waiting for him stateside, Derrick did several tours overseas.

While in the army, Derrick starts to drink. He is sober when he is on duty. But as soon as he is off duty, with his army buddies, they find the nearest bar. Even though Derrick drinks more than most of his buddies, he is the quickest to rebound and jump out of bed the following day.

Derrick is stationed at Fort Carson in Colorado at the end of his enlistment and decides to remain in Colorado. A month before he was released from the army, he met a wonderful woman who reminded him a lot of his mom. Within a short period, he proposes, and they are married. Their daughter is born several years later.

Though Derrick is now married with a child, he continues drinking with his army buddies. His wife asks him to stop drinking, to get help, and go to counseling. Derrick doesn't see any need to seek counseling. He isn't an alcoholic like his dad. He just needs a drink with his buddies to unwind after his day ends working as a chauffeur.

Sitting on the barstool, Derrick entertains his friends with stories about the rich and famous he chauffeured that day. He likes to hear his friends laugh. He likes to be the one who tells the stories that have his friends laughing and entertained.

One day when Derrick returns home from the bar after yet another night of drinking with his buddies, the house is strangely dark and quiet. As Derrick turns on the light, he finds an empty house. Nothing is left. All the furniture is gone. The only things left behind are his clothes hanging in the closet all by themselves.

In disbelief, Derrick wanders the empty house. He finds a note on the refrigerator door telling him that since he was unwilling to admit he is an alcoholic or go to counseling, she was left with only one choice. That choice is to relocate herself and their daughter to some place safe, away from him.

In the note, she tells him there would be no way for him to find her. None of her friends know where she has gone or even that she has left.

For months Derrick tries to find his wife and daughter. Both of her parents had already died. Being an only child like himself, she didn't have any siblings he could call to find out where they had gone.

He tells no one of their disappearances. He believes she will return. She will reach out. Yet, she never does.

Over the years, he drinks more and more to deaden the pain he feels inside. The emptiness he feels is unbearable. He feels powerless against the alcohol. He doesn't want to feel anything, particularly the heartache and emptiness.

The bar, the barstool, and drinking become a way of life for him. He still entertains everyone at the bar with stories about the rich and famous, yet he feels very alone and lonely.

He had sworn he would never be like his dad, yet he turned out just like him. He feels insignificant, unworthy, and undeserving. He feels he is without hope, his life is hopeless, and he isn't worth saving.

No one at work knows he is an alcoholic. He is always sober at work. Can't drink and drive. After his shift ends, he is back on his barstool, entertaining his friends. It feels as if alcohol is his best friend. He doesn't know any other way to be.

One wintry, lonely November night, as he sits on the barstool, Derrick feels as if he has squandered his life away. He feels hollow and shallow and that his life has no purpose. Derrick doesn't feel he is worthy of being loved, and maybe it is time to end his life.

He has nothing to live for. He is a drunk. He can't remember a day in hasn't had at least one drink. As he walks home one lonely night, he thinks about ending the pain by ending his life.

The next day, he drives another rich and famous person. Derrick wanders into the library as he waits for his guest. He ends up in the self-help, success, and motivation section. He pulls books off the shelf, carries them to a comfy chair, and starts reading.

Derrick drives the same guest to the same event for the next three days, and each day he walks to the library and reads. After returning the car to the garage the final night, he checks his schedule in the office.

It is late, and everyone has left for the day except Sarah, who is finishing up the schedule. Sarah tells Derrick she will have his schedule in a jiffy and to have a seat.

On Sarah's desk is a book on the success that Derrick just browsed that day at the library. He picks up the book and starts to read. Derrick doesn't notice when Sarah finishes the schedule. She laughs and asks if Derrick would like his schedule.

"Is this your secret?" he asks.

"My secret to what?" responds Sarah.

Derrick had always been impressed at how calm Sarah was. He knows her life is hectic with a husband deployed overseas, three children to raise on her own, and a full-time job. "To being at peace all the time," Derrick says.

She laughs at the thought of someone thinking of her at peace. "Well, I like reading motivational books. It wasn't too long ago that my life was a mess!"

Derrick can't help but be surprised. "You? Is your life a mess? Unbelievable."

"It's true. I was an alcoholic. No one knew. I kept it hidden from everyone. I couldn't keep it a secret for long when I got married. Because I could keep it from my husband when we dated, I thought I would be able to keep it from him when we married. Not so easy when you live with someone.

"I had an alcoholic mom. I told myself I would never be like my mom. I gave myself many 'reasons,' or should I say 'excuses,' for drinking. My mom had told me I would never amount to much. I felt incomplete and inadequate. I didn't feel I had the tools or skills to be successful at anything."

With interest, Derrick looks quizzically at Sarah and asks, "Reading these books, is this how you turned your life around?"

"Well, actually not totally. My husband gave me an ultimatum: our marriage or the bottle. I chose marriage. Fortunately, a friend of mine had just started practice as an EFT Tapping practitioner. With her help, I could change the beliefs that led to my drinking. I dealt with my shame, guilt, apathy, fear, and anger."

"Do you think I could have her phone number?" asks Derrick.

"Sure." Derrick slides the phone number into his pocket.

Later that night, as Derrick is sitting on his barstool, he feels as if the phone number is burning a hole in his pants' pocket. Every morning as Derrick leaves for work, he slides the phone number into his pocket, thinking he might call that day.

Even though he wants to heal his addiction to alcohol, he thinks it is too late for him. Even though he wants to heal his black, empty heart, he doesn't think anything could ever take away the pain and fill the emptiness. Even though he is tired of feeling separate from everything and everyone, he doesn't believe anything could change the way he has felt his whole life.

Sitting on the barstool night after night had become his life, his identity. He doesn't believe a counselor could bring him back from the dead. There is no happiness to be found inside. He is still bitter and angry that his wife has abandoned him and taken his daughter away from him. He also knew he was afraid to find out if anything was inside.

Several weeks later, Sarah asks Derrick if he has called her friend. Derrick pulls the crumpled paper out of his pocket and admits he had not. Every day he carries the number with him, but he doesn't dare to call or start down a path of more pain.

"Derrick, it sounds like you are in pain. If you are already in pain, what harm could it do?"

Sarah picks up the phone, dials the number, and hands Derrick the phone. He schedules an appointment for the following week.

The following week Derrick approaches Sarah's desk and asks if he could sit down. "I want to thank you for calling your friend and handing me the phone."

"How did your appointment go?" asks Sarah with genuine interest.

"I have never had to face myself. You know, really look deep inside. I don't like what I see. But, for the first time in my life, I feel there just might be some hope for me," says Derrick.

"Is there anything I can do to help?" asks Sarah.

"Be my friend and be a sounding board from time to time," responds Derrick.

"That I can do!" beamed Sarah.

Each week for six months, Derrick stops by to chat with Sarah after his appointment with the EFT practitioner. Being open and authentic is a challenge for Derrick. However, he wants to "practice" being authentic with someone who would not be judgmental, has been where he is now, and came out on the other side of hell to happiness.

One day Derrick is excited to chat with Sarah. "I owe you a huge debt of gratitude!"

Sarah stops what she is doing, looks up at Derrick, and asks why.

"My daughter contacted me last night and wants to come to visit me. If I had not been working on myself, doing the EFT Tapping, there is no way I would have been comfortable spending time with her. I would have been embarrassed for her to see the man I was. Now I like myself. I have a life. I am proud of myself. I came out of hell to happiness, and that's the man my daughter will meet."

Sarah is thrilled Derrick is so happy and that EFT Tapping had been an answer for him as well.

Before Derrick meets with his daughter, he taps. He does a lot of tapping until he knows he could be his authentic self around his daughter. At first, it was intimidating. He doesn't know what to say or how to explain the past.

However, his daughter is quick to put him at ease, and the hours fly by as they get to know each other. Derrick is excited when she tells her dad that she has decided to attend college nearby so they can get to know each other.

He feels eternally grateful to EFT Tapping, Sarah, and his practitioner, who helped him find his joy and for the blissful reunion with his daughter.

EFT
TAPPING

Chapter 3
EFT Tapping - Emotional Freedom Technique

EFT Tapping is a very easy technique to learn. It involves making a statement as we contact the body by either circling or tapping.

An EFT Tapping Statement has three parts:

Part 1: starts with "**Even though**" followed by

Part 2: a statement which could be the **dysfunctional emotion or belief**, and

Part 3: ends with "**I totally and completely accept myself.**"

A complete statement would be, "**Even though I fear change, I totally and completely accept myself.**"

Instruction for the Short Form of EFT Tapping

The instructions below are for using the right hand. Reverse the directions to tap using the left hand. It is more effective, when we tap, to tap only one side rather than both.

I. Set up - begin with circling or tapping the Side of the Hand:

A. With the fingertips of the right hand, find a tender spot below the left collar bone. Once the tender spot is identified, press firmly on the spot, moving the fingertips in a circular motion toward the left shoulder, toward the outside, clockwise. Tapping the side of the hand can also be used instead of the circling.

B. As the fingers circle and press against the tender spot or tap the side of the hand, repeat the tapping statement three times: "Even though, [tapping statement] , I totally and completely accept myself." An example would be: "Even though I fear change, I totally and completely accept myself."

Side of the hand

Tender spot below the left collar bone

II. TAPPING:

A. After the third time, tap the following eight points, repeating the [tapping statement] at each point. Tap each point five – ten times:

1. The inner edge of the eyebrow, just above the eye. [I fear change.]
2. Temple, just to the side of the eye. [I fear change.]
3. Just below the eye (on the cheekbone). [I fear change.]
4. Under the nose. [I fear change.]
5. Under the lips. [I fear change.]
6. Under the knob of the collar bone. [I fear change.]
7. Three inches under the arm pit. [I fear change.]
8. Top back of the head. [I fear change.]

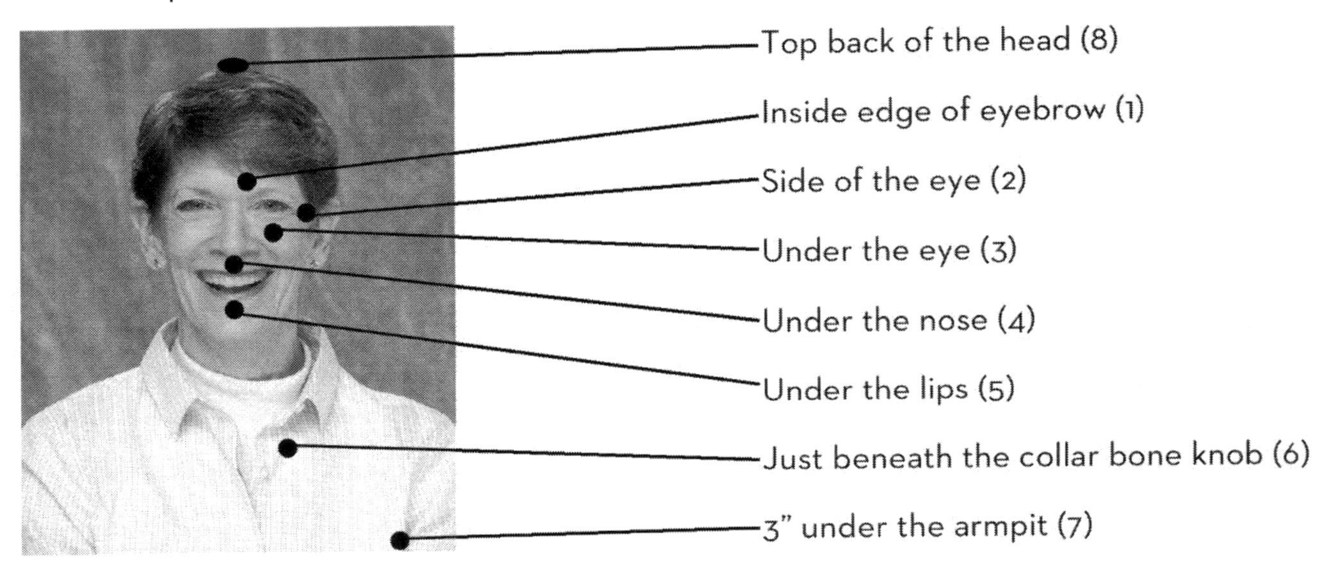

B. After tapping, take a deep breath. If you are not able to take a deep, full, satisfying breath, do eye rolls.

III. EYE ROLLS

A. With one hand tap continuously on the **back** of the other hand between the fourth and fifth fingers.
B. Hold your head straight forward, eyes looking straight down.
C. For six seconds, roll your eyes from the floor straight up toward the ceiling while repeating the tapping statement. Keep the head straight forward, only moving the eyes.

IV. TAKE ANOTHER DEEP BREATH.

Chapter 4
EFT Tapping, Beliefs, and the Subconscious Mind

EFT - Emotional Freedom Technique

EFT is a technique that allows us to change dysfunctional beliefs and emotions on a subconscious level. It involves making a statement while tapping different points along meridian paths.

The general principle behind EFT is that the cause of all negative emotions is a disruption in the body's energy system. By tapping on locations where several different meridians flow, we can release unproductive memories, emotions, and beliefs that cause the blockages.

A Belief is...

A belief is a mental acceptance of, and conviction in, the Truth, actuality, or validity of something. It is what we believe to be true, whether it is Truth or not. A belief is a thought that influences energy all the time.

A Dysfunctional Belief is...

A dysfunctional belief is a belief that takes us away from peace, love, joy, stability, acceptance, and harmony. It causes us to feel stressed, fearful, anxious, and/or insecure.

The Conscious Mind is...

The conscious mind is the part of us that thinks, passes judgments, makes decisions, remembers, analyzes, has desires, and communicates with others. It is responsible for logic and reasoning, understanding and comprehension. The mind determines our actions, feelings, thoughts, judgments, and decisions **based on beliefs.**

The Subconscious Mind is...

The subconscious is the part of the mind responsible for all our involuntary actions like our heartbeat and breathing rate. It does not evaluate, make decisions, or pass judgment. It just is. It does not determine if something is "right" or "wrong."

The subconscious is much like the software of a computer. On the computer keyboard, if we press the key for the letter "a," we will see the letter "a" on the screen, even though we may have wanted to see "t." Just as a computer can only do what it has been programmed to do, we can only do as we are programmed to do.

Our programming is determined by our beliefs. Beliefs and memories are "stored" in the subconscious.

Three Rules of the Subconscious Mind

Three rules of the subconscious mind include:

1. Personal. It only understands "I," "me," "myself." First-person.
2. Positive. The subconscious does not hear the word "no." When you say, "I am not going to eat that piece of cake," the subconscious mind hears, "Yummm! Cake! I am going to eat a piece of that cake!"
3. Present time. Time does not exist for the subconscious. The only time it knows is "now," present time. "I'm going to start my diet tomorrow." "Tomorrow" never comes; thus, the diet never starts.

Beliefs precede all of our thoughts, feelings,
decisions, choices, actions, reactions,
and experiences...

Our beliefs and memories are stored
in the subconscious mind.

If we want to make changes in our lives,
we have to change the programming,
the dysfunctional beliefs in the subconscious.

Three rules of the Subconscious Mind:
Personal
Positive
Present time

Chapter 5
How Does EFT Tapping Work?

1. Acceptance: The last part of the tapping statement, we say, "I totally and completely accept myself." **Acceptance brings us into present time.** We can only heal if we are in present time.

2. Addresses the current dysfunctional beliefs on a subconscious level: To make changes in our lives, we have to change the dysfunctional beliefs on a subconscious level. The middle part of the tapping statements are the "instructions" for the subconscious. **To make changes in our lives, we only care what the subconscious hears.**

3. Pattern interrupt: Dysfunctional memories and/or beliefs block energy from flowing freely along the meridians. Tapping is a pattern interrupt that disrupts the flow of energy to allow our **body's own Infinite Wisdom to come forth for healing.** (Tapping both sides does not act as a pattern interrupt.)

4. Mis-direct: One role of the physical body is to protect us. When our hand is too close to a flame, our body automatically pulls our hand back to safety. An EFT Tapping statement that agrees with the current belief is more effective. The physical body is less likely to sabotage the tapping if it agrees with the current belief.

For the EFT Taping statement "I fear change":

* This statement appeases the physical body since it agrees with the current belief.
* The tapping disrupts the energy flow so our Truth can come forth.

The body will always gravitate to health, wealth, and well-being when the conditions allow it. EFT Tapping weeds the garden so the blossoms can bloom more easily and effortlessly.

Chapter 6
Benefits of Using EFT Tapping

* The last part of the statement is, "I totally and completely **accept** myself." **Acceptance** brings us into present time. Healing can only take place when we are in present time.

* By tapping, we are **calling forth our Truths**. The keyword here is "**our**." Not anyone else's. If my name is "Lucas," tapping the statement "Even though my name is Troy," my name will not change to Troy.

* Tapping **calls forth our body's Infinite Wisdom**. When we cut our finger, our body knows how to heal the cut itself. Once the dysfunctional emotions, experiences, and beliefs have been "deleted," our body **automatically** gravitates to health, wealth, wisdom, peace, love, joy...

* By changing dysfunctional beliefs and emotions on a subconscious level, the changes we make with EFT are **permanent.**

* EFT Tapping can change:
  Beliefs
  Emotions
  Self-images
  Our story
  Thoughts
  Mind chatter
  Painful memories

* EFT Tapping can neutralize stored memories that block energy along the meridians.

* EFT Tapping can desensitize emotions. We might have a difficult person in our life who ignores us and/or criticizes us, so we tap the statement: "This difficult person [or their name] ignores and criticizes me."

  Tapping does not mean they will no longer ignore and/or criticize us; however, it can **desensitize us,** so we are no longer affected by their behavior. Once we have desensitized the emotions, our perception and mental thinking improve. We are better able to make informed decisions. We don't take and make everything personal. Our health is not negatively impacted. Our heart doesn't beat 100 beats/minute. Smoke stops coming out of our ears, and our faces don't turn red with anger and frustration.

Chapter 7
What We Say As We Tap Is VERY Important!

All of our beliefs are programmed into our subconscious minds. If we want to change our lives, we have to delete the dysfunctional beliefs on a subconscious level. The statements we make as we tap are the instructions for the subconscious mind.

THE TAPPING STATEMENTS WE WAY AS WE ARE TAPPING ARE CRITICAL FOR THIS TO HAPPEN!

Example: You get in a taxi. Several hours later, you still have not arrived at your destination. "*Why?*" you ask. Because you did not give the destination to the taxi driver!

Tapping without saying an adequate tapping statement is like riding in a cab without giving the cab driver our destination!

For EFT Tapping to be MOST EFFECTIVE the Tapping Statement is CRITICAL!

EFT Tapping allows us to delete the dysfunctional beliefs on a subconscious level. The statements we make as we tap are instructions to the subconscious mind so our Truth can come forth.

Chapter 8
Using a Negative EFT Tapping Statement

Our beliefs **precede** all of our thoughts, feelings, decisions, choices, actions, reactions, and experiences.

If we want to make changes in our lives, we have to change the dysfunctional beliefs. Our beliefs are stored in the subconscious.

To change our lives, to change a belief, we only care what the subconscious hears when we tap. The subconscious does not hear the word "no." When we say, "I am not going to eat that piece of cake," the subconscious hears, "Yummm, cake!"

Example, if we don't believe we have what it takes to be successful and we tap the statement, "I have what it takes to be successful," the body could sabotage the tapping. We could tap and it won't clear.

Instead, if the statement we make is, "I do not have what it takes to be successful," the "**not**" appeases the physical body and the subconscious hears, "I have what it takes to be successful!"

Chapter 9
EFT Tapping Statements Are Most Effective When They Agree With Current Beliefs

The EFT Tapping statement is **more successful when** it **is something the body currently believes.**

The body is less likely to sabotage an EFT Tapping statement that agrees with the current belief.

One role of the physical body is to protect us from harm. (For example, if our hand gets too close to a flame, our body will pull our hand back to safety.) The body is less likely to sabotage the statement and the process if the EFT Tapping statement agrees with the current belief. Thus, it appeases the physical body.

For example, if our desire is prosperity and wealth and we tap the statement, "I am prosperous now," the body could sabotage the tapping by forgetting what we were saying, getting easily distracted, or our mind chatter may remind us we are not prosperous. We could tap and the statement, most likely, will not clear.

If the statement we say is "I am not prosperous now," the "**not**" appeases the physical body, and the subconscious hears, "I am prosperous now!"

Chapter 10
The Very First EFT Tapping Statement to Tap

The very first EFT Tapping statement I have clients and students tap is, "It is not okay or safe for my life to change." I have muscle tested this statement with more than a thousand people. Not one person tested strong that it was okay or safe for their life to change. (Muscle testing is a way in which we can converse with the body, bypassing the conscious mind.)

How effective can EFT or any therapy be if it is not okay or safe for our lives to change?

Since our lives are constantly changing, if it is not okay or safe for our lives to change, every time our lives change, it creates stress for the body. Stress creates another whole set of issues for ourselves, our lives, and our bodies.

Chapter 11
One Statement per Round of EFT vs Multiple Statements per Round of EFT

Laser-focused Tapping vs Round Robin Tapping

Same Statement for all the Tapping Points in One Round vs Multiple Statements in One Round of Tapping (Scripts)

Two styles of tapping for different purposes. One style is best for healing dysfunctional beliefs. The other style is best for healing emotions, desensitizing a story, situation, and/or memory.

I found that the laser-focused, one statement for a round of tapping was most effective for healing the beliefs. Multiple statements per round of tapping is great at healing emotions, desensitizing a story, situation, and/or memory.

Same Statement for All the Tapping Points in One Round

After tapping the statement, "It's not okay for my life to change," and we are able to take a deep breath, we know the statement cleared. Then we tap, "I'm not ready for my life to change," and we are not able to take a deep breath, most likely, the statement did not clear.

Knowing the statement did not clear, we can focus on the reasons, excuses, and/or beliefs about not being ready to change our lives.

* Maybe the changes we need to make would require more of us than we want to give.
* Maybe we don't feel we have the abilities we would need if our life changed.
* Maybe we don't feel our support system, the people in our life, would support the changes we want to make.

Follow-up tapping statements for "I'm not ready for my life to change" could be:

* I do not have the abilities change would require.
* I am afraid of change.
* Others will not support the changes I want to make in my life.
* I am not able to make the changes I want to make.
* I do not have the courage that change would require.
* I am too old to change.

Tapping the same statement at all eight points is most effective for clearing beliefs. When a statement does not clear, we can focus on the reasons, excuses, and/or dysfunctional beliefs that blocked the statement from clearing.

Multiple Statements in One Round of Tapping (Scripts/Round Robin)

Tapping multiple statements in one round, also known as Scripts or Round Robin tapping, is excellent for healing a story, and desensitizing a memory or story.

Healing a broken heart, to desensitize the heartache of the break up, the following script/statements could be said, one statement/point:

* My boyfriend broke up with me.
* I am heartbroken.
* He said he doesn't love me anymore.
* I do not know how I can go on without him.
* It hurts.
* I am sad he doesn't love me anymore.
* I am sad our relationship is over.
* I will never find anyone like him ever again.

Reframing:

Reframing is a Neuro Linguistic Programming (NLP) term. It is a way to view and experience emotions, situations, and/or behaviors in a more positive manner.

At the end of round robin tapping, we can introduce statements to "reframe" the situation.

An example of reframing could be:

* I want this chocolate.
* Maybe eating chocolate is wanting to reconnect to my childhood.
* Maybe eating sugar is a way of being loved.
* Maybe I can find a different way of being loved.

Round robin tapping, scripts, can desensitize the hurt and pain. It can heal the pain of our story. It may not rewrite the beliefs. To clear out the beliefs, it would be necessary to look at the reasons the relationship didn't work and why our heart is broken, or why we crave chocolate.

Round robin/script tapping can also be done by just tapping the side of the hand.

Side of Hand Tapping to Desensitize a Story, Situation, and/or Memory

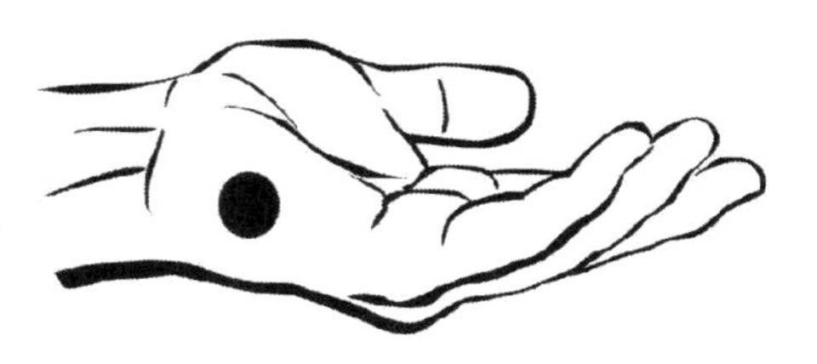

Just as in the round robin tapping/scripts, we said different statements, one after the other, we can say the same statements and just tap the side of the hand.

If a memory still "haunts" us, embarrasses us, and/or affects our actions in any way, this technique might be perfect to neutralize the memory.

For example:

As Sasha remembers the first dance she attended as a teen-ager, tears well up in her eyes. She starts to tap the side of the hand (SOH) as she tells her story:

My best friend, Samantha and I, were so excited about attending our first high school dance. We weren't old enough to drive so Sam's dad dropped us off in front of the high school auditorium where the dance was held.

(Continue to tap the SOH) We were in awe of how the auditorium was transformed into a palace. Sofas were placed around a hardwood dance floor in the center of the room. We promised each other we would be there for the other throughout the night so neither of us would be stranded alone.

(Continue to tap the SOH) Well, along came Billy McDaniels. Sam had had a crush on Billy since third grade. He asked her to dance and I never saw her again for the rest of the night.

(Continue to tap the SOH) Those three hours were probably the worst night of my entire life! No one asked me to dance. Every time I joined a group of girls, a new song would begin, and every one of them was asked to dance, everyone except me. I don't know why no one asked me to dance. I felt ugly, abandoned, and undesirable! Talk about being a wallflower. I thought I was invisible. I wanted to hide from embarrassment.

(Continue to tap the SOH) This was back in the days before cell phones. The auditorium didn't have a payphone to call my parents to come and get me. I had to endure three hours of humiliation watching every single girl be asked to dance EXCEPT me.

(Continue to tap the SOH) I never attended another high school dance again!

Whether we tap the side of the hand or the eight tapping points, the result is the same. Round robin tapping can desensitize emotions and memories very effectively.

There are different styles of EFT Tapping.
Find the style that works best for your desired result.

Chapter 12
Walking Backwards EFT (Backing Up)

As I was working with a client, they had an issue that was not clearing. Knowing that movement helps to clear issues, I decided to have the person stand up and walk backward. Literally, walk backward, step after step, facing forward while their feet moved backward.

Surprise, surprise, it worked. Every statement cleared as she backed up.

The next client came in. I had him walk backwards, and it worked with clearing issues for him as well. Both clients were somewhat athletic and did workout. I wanted to know if the Backing Up would work with non-athletic people. I was teaching an EFT class the next day. At the end of the class, we all backed up together. And, IT WORKED!

Let's say we want to process, "I will never be comfortable in the world." Stand up. Make sure nothing is behind you. Then walk backward while facing forward and say, "I will never be comfortable in the world. I will never be comfortable in the world. I will never be comfortable in the world. I will never be comfortable in the world." Repeat the phrase six - eight times.

When we back up, we say the same statement we would have made if we were tapping. We don't have to say the "Even though" or the last remainder phrase, "I totally and completely accept myself."

Walking forward represents forward movement in our lives. Walking backward represents the past.

Physical movement can help clear emotional issues and facilitate change.

Walking backward undoes the past and helps to clear, heal, and transform an issue in our lives.

Chapter 13
Intensity Level

One measure of knowing how much an issue has been resolved is to begin, before tapping, by giving the issue an intensity number (IL) between 1 and 10, with 10 being high.

For example, we want a romantic partnership, yet we haven't met "the one." Thinking about a romantic relationship happening, what is the likelihood, on a scale of 1 - 10, with 10 being very likely and 1, not likely at all, of a romantic relationship happening?

Okay. We give ourselves a 2. Now, let's start tapping!

When asked what the issues might be, "Well," we say, "it does not seem as if the people who I want, want me."

Great tapping statement. Tap, "Even though the people I want don't want me, I totally and completely accept myself." After tapping, we check in with ourselves; the IL has gone up to a 4, so it is now a little bit more likely.

What comes to mind now? "No one will find me desirable." Great tapping statement. "Even though no one will find me desirable, I totally and completely accept myself." Check the IL. How likely? 5. Cool! Progress.

What comes to mind now? "I'm not comfortable being vulnerable in romantic relationships." Great tapping statement. "Even though I'm not comfortable being vulnerable in a romantic relationship, I totally and completely accept myself." Check the IL. Now it is a 6. Still progress.

What comes to mind now? "Well, it feels like if I am in a relationship, I will lose a lot of my freedom." Make this into a tapping statement. "Even though I will lose my freedom when I am in a relationship, I totally and completely accept myself." The IL has gone up to a 7.

What comes to mind now? "Oh, if I was in a relationship, I would have to be accountable to someone!" Make this into a tapping statement: "Even though, I would have to be accountable to someone if I was in a relationship, I totally and completely accept myself." Wow...the IL is 9, very likely!

Giving an issue an Intensity Level gives at the beginning and throughout the session gives us an indication of the progress we are making with resolving and/or healing that issue in our lives.

Chapter 14
Yawning and Taking a Deep Breath

From Traditional Chinese Medicine, we know that when chi (energy) flows freely through the meridians, the body is healthy and balanced. Physical, mental, and/or emotional illness can result when the energy is blocked.

Dysfunctional beliefs and emotions produce blocks along the meridians, blocking energy from flowing freely in the body.

With EFT Tapping, as we tap, we release the blocks. As blocked energy is able to flow more freely, the body can now "breathe a sigh of relief." Yawning is that sigh of relief.

If, after tapping, we can take a complete, deep, full, and satisfying breath, we know that an EFT Tapping statement has cleared. This yawn is an indication that an EFT Tapping statement has cleared.

If the yawn or breath is not a full, deep breath then the statement did not clear completely.

Chapter 15
Integration...What Happens After Tapping

After tapping, our system needs some downtime for integration to take place. When the physical body and the mind are "idle," integration can take place.

Sometimes, in the first 24 hours after tapping, we might find ourselves vegging more than normal, sleeping more than normal, or more tired than normal. This downtime is needed to integrate the new changes.

After installing a new program into our computer, sometimes we have to reboot the computer (shut down and restart) for the new program to be integrated into the system.

After tapping, our bodies need to reboot. We need some downtime. When we sleep, the new changes are integrated.

HEALING BEGINS NATURALLY AFTER THE BODY HAS HAD A CHANCE TO INTEGRATE.

Sometimes, after tapping, we forget the intensity of our pain and think that feeling better had nothing to do with tapping. Something so simple could not possibly create the improvement in our state of mind!

When we cut our finger, once it is healed, we don't even remember cutting our finger. As we move toward health, wealth, and well-being, sometimes we don't remember how unhappy, restless, or isolated we once felt.

Chapter 16
EFT Tapping Doesn't Work for Me

Why might EFT Tapping not be working?

* The tapping statement might not be worded such that a dysfunctional belief and/or emotion is addressed and eliminated.
* The style (laser-focused style vs round robin) of tapping may not be effective for the statement to be cleared.
* The EFT Tapping statement is only addressing a symptom and **not the cause of the issue.**

FOR EFT TAPPING TO BE EFFECTIVE, THE CAUSE OF THE ISSUE NEEDS TO BE HEALED.

* Having an awareness of our issues does not heal the dysfunctional beliefs.
* Forgiving ourselves and/or someone else does not heal the dysfunctional beliefs.
* Talk therapy does not heal the dysfunctional beliefs.
* Desensitizing the emotions does not heal the dysfunctional beliefs.
* Healing the experience of a hurtful event does not change the dysfunctional beliefs.

EFT Tapping works best when

1) the statements are worded to eliminate the dysfunctional beliefs,
2) the most effective style of tapping is utilized, and
3) we are healing the cause, not just the symptoms.

Chapter 17
What to Do if an EFT Tapping Statement Does Not Clear

When a statement might not clear, turn the statement into a question. The statement, "It's not okay for me to be powerful," didn't clear. **Turn the tapping statement into a question:** "Why isn't it okay for me to be powerful?"

The answer might be:

* Powerful people are ruthless and heartless.
* I am afraid of being powerful.
* Being powerful would change me for the worse.
* Power corrupts.
* People would laugh at me if I tried being powerful.
* I would have to give up my fears and anxieties to be powerful.
* I might be called aggressive if I tried being powerful.
* I do not have the abilities, skills, or qualities to be powerful.
* Others would make fun of me if I tried being powerful.
* Powerful people are thoughtless and self-centered.

With these beliefs, it might not be okay or safe to be powerful or even explore the idea of being powerful. The statements above are tapping statements. Tap the answer to the question.

After tapping the answer to the question, revisit the original statement that did not clear. Most likely, it will now be cleared, and you will be able to take a full, deep, and complete breath.

Chapter 18
Science and EFT Tapping Research

EFT has been researched in more than ten countries by more than sixty investigators whose results have been published in more than twenty different peer-reviewed journals. Two leading researchers are Dawson Church, Ph.D. and David Feinstein, Ph.D.

Dr. Dawson Church, a leading expert on energy psychology and an EFT master, has gathered all the research information, and it can be found on this website: www.EFTUniverse.com.

Two Research Studies

1) Harvard Medical School Studies and the Brain's Stress Response

Studies at the Harvard Medical School reveal that stimulating the body's meridian points significantly reduces activity in a part of the brain called the amygdala.

The amygdala can be thought of as the body's alarm system. When the body is experiencing trauma or fear, the amygdala is triggered, and the body is flooded with cortisol, also known as the stress hormone. The stress response sets up an intricate chain reaction.

The studies showed that stimulating or tapping points along the meridians such as EFT Tapping, drastically reduced and/or eliminated the stress response and the resulting chain reaction.

2) Dr. Dawson Church and Cortisol Reduction

Another significant study was conducted by Dr. Dawson Church. He studied the impact an hour's tapping session had on the cortisol levels of eighty-three subjects. He also measured the cortisol levels of people who received traditional talk therapy and those of a third group who received no treatment at all.

On average, for the eighty-three subjects who completed an hour tapping session, cortisol levels were reduced by 24%. Some subjects experienced a 50% reduction in cortisol levels.

The subjects who completed one hour of traditional talk therapy and those who had completed neither session did not experience any significant cortisol reduction.

Chapter 19
Is Lowering the Cortisol Level Enough to Permanently Change Our Lives?

Several things can lower our cortisol (stress hormone) levels including:
* Power posing
* Meditating
* Laughing
* Exercising regularly
* Listening to music
* Getting a massage
* Eliminating caffeine from our diet
* Eating a balanced, nutritious meal and eliminating processed food

Would performing any of the above activities lower our cortisol level enough to permanently change our lives? Only if the activity eliminates the dysfunctional beliefs on a subconscious level.

All of our thoughts, feelings, actions, reactions, choices, and decisions are preceded by a belief. To change our lives, the dysfunctional beliefs must be eliminated.

Power posing, listening to music, or eating a balanced meal will not permanently change our lives. Exercising will help our physical body but will not delete our dysfunctional beliefs. Laughing will bring us into the present so we will not be drawn into our fears or anger, but it will not change our lives. Meditating helps us to center and balance, but will not change our lives on a permanent basis.

To change our lives, we must be able to recognize, acknowledge, and take ownership of that which we want to change then delete the dysfunctional emotions and beliefs that preceded that what we want to change on a subconscious level.

EFT Tapping will delete dysfunctional emotions and beliefs on a subconscious level if we provide the correct "instructions" to our subconscious mind. We must word the tapping statements in the subconscious' language. We must word the tapping statement so the subconscious mind hears what we want to eliminate.

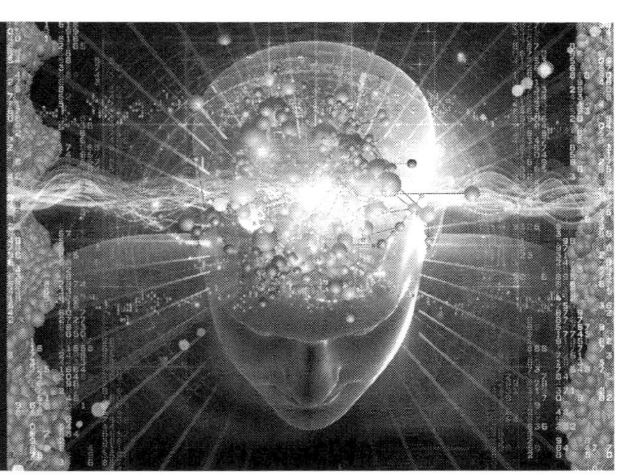

Chapter 20
Tapping Affirmations

* I am healthy and happy.
* Wealth is pouring into my life.
* I radiate love and happiness.
* I have the perfect job for me.
* I am successful in whatever I do.

If we were to tap "I am healthy and happy now" and we are not, most likely, as we are tapping, we might think, "Yeah, right. Sure. I am healthy and happy. My life sucks. I hate my job. I am always broke. There is never enough money..."

The body knows this is not true. We are not healthy and happy now. When we tap, we might have difficulty remembering what we are saying, lose focus and concentration, and/or the mind drifts.

An EFT Tapping statement is most effective **when** it matches our current belief.

The subconscious does not hear the word "No." One way of tapping affirmations and, at the same time, putting in the positives is to put the word "no" into the tapping statements.

* I am **not** healthy and happy. Subconscious hears: I am healthy and happy.
* Wealth is **not** pouring into my life. Subconscious hears: Wealth is pouring into my life.
* I **do not** radiate love and happiness. Subconscious hears: I radiate love and happiness.
* I **do not** have the perfect job for me. Subconscious hears: I have the perfect job for me.
* I am **not** successful in whatever I do. Subconscious hears: I am successful in whatever I do.

If we repeat affirmations over and over and over before we clear the affirmation with EFT Tapping, repeating the affirmation numerous times will have little effect except to create circumstances in our lives so we can be confronted with the beliefs that do not align with the affirmation.

Chapter 21
Finishing Touches - Positive Statements

Some like to finish their tapping with statements that are centering and calming. If this is you, then you might want to try the 16 statements on the next page or make up those that you like. The statements can be said in any order that works for you.

Tapping Location	Statement
Eyebrow	All is well in my life.
Temple	Every day in every way
Under the Eye	I am fulfilled in every way, every day.
Under the Nose	My blessings appears in rich
Under the Lips	I am an excellent steward of wealth and am blessed with great abundance.
Under the Collarbone Knob	I take complete responsibility
Under the Arm	I have all the tools, skills, and
Top back part of the Head	I know I will be able to handle anything
Eyebrow	All my dreams, hopes, wishes, and goals
Temple	Divine love expressing through me,
Under the Eye	I am comfortable with my life changing.
Under the Nose	I am able to create all that I desire.
Under the Lips	I know what needs to be done and
Under the Collarbone Knob	My health is perfect in every way, physically,
Under the Arm	I invite into my subconscious Archangel Raphael to heal all that needs to be forgiven, released, and redeemed. Cleanse me and free me from it now.
Top back part of the Head	The light of God surrounds me. The love of God enfolds me. The power of God protects me. The presence of God watches over and flows through me.

Chapter 22
How to Use This Book

1. The statements are divided into sections. Read through the statements in one section. As you read a statement, notice if you have any reaction to the statement or feel the statement might be true for you. If so, note the number for that statement.

2. Once you have completed reading all the statements in one section, go back and reread the statements you noted and rate them on a scale of 1 - 10, with 10 being a "biggie."

3. List the top statements.

4. From this list, select one and describe how it plays out in your life. It is important to recognize and identify the pattern. What are the consequences of having this belief? Is there a trigger? How does it begin? How does it benefit you? How has it harmed you? There will be a different example listed in each section.

5. Tap the statements. Statements can be combined for scripts...a different statement on each of the different tapping points in one round of tapping.

6. Describe any flashbacks or memories that you might have had as you were tapping out the statements. Describe any ah-has, insights, and/or thoughts you might have had as a result of tapping the statements.

7. After tapping all the statements, review them to determine if you still have a reaction to any of the statements. If you do, you have several options. One, put a "Why" before the statement. Tap out the answer. Secondly, note that this statement may not have cleared and continue on to the next section. Most likely, after additional statements are tapped, statements that may not have cleared, will clear without having to tap the statement again.

8. Allow some downtime for integration and for the body to heal.

9. The number of sections you do at a time will be up to you. Initially, you might want to do one section to determine if you get tired and need to have some downtime after tapping.

10. The day after tapping, again review the statements you tapped to determine if you still have a reaction. If you do, follow the instructions in #7.

1 – 20 EFT Tapping Statements

Better shun the bait than struggle in the snare.

John Dryden

1. I am not lovable.
2. I feel dead inside.
3. My life is hopeless.
4. I prefer to be alone.
5. I am a fake and fraud.
6. Denial keeps me safe.
7. I am not worth saving.
8. I am afraid of intimacy.
9. I feel alone and lonely.
10. My life has no purpose.
11. I don't matter or count.
12. I squander my life away.
13. I can't transform my life.
14. I didn't matter as a child.
15. I don't belong anywhere.
16. I feel hollow and shallow.
17. I lack emotional courage.
18. I feel small and powerless.
19. I don't feel worthy of love.
20. I was very lonely as a child.

Journaling Pages for Statements 1 - 20

People spend a lifetime searching for happiness; looking for peace. They chase idle dreams, addictions, religions, even other people, hoping to fill the emptiness that plagues them. The irony is the only place they ever needed to search was within.

Ramona L. Anderson

1. From the tapping statements between 1 - 20, list the top seven statements that you thought or felt applied to you:

1.

2.

3.

4.

5.

6.

7.

2. From this list of seven statements, select one and describe how it plays out in your life. Give an example or two. It is important to recognize and identify the pattern. Is there a trigger? How does it begin? How has it benefited you? How has it harmed you? For instance, if you looked within, would you find happiness? Or is happiness dependent on something outside of you?

3. Tap out the top 7 statements.

4. As you were tapping out the statements, did you have any flashback or memories of the past, any additional insights, and/or ah-ha thoughts? If so, write them down. Make note of them.

21 - 40 EFT Tapping Statements

Opportunity may knock only once.
Temptation leans on the doorbell.

Unknown

21. I blame others for my addiction.
22. I don't live the life I want to live.
23. I need my addiction to feel safe.
24. I know I am wasting my life but...
25. My future looks and is hopeless.
26. I am drowning in my depression.
27. I need to be right and in control.
28. I make excuses for my addiction.
29. I am not a good friend to myself.
30. It isn't safe to reveal the real me.
31. I need my addiction to be happy.
32. I don't know if I am worth saving.
33. My wounds are too deep to heal.
34. I don't know any other way to be.
35. I don't know how to heal my pain.
36. I crave normalcy and consistency.
37. I am destructive, mean, and cruel.
38. Something is broken inside of me.
39. I feel different from other people.
40. I can't handle the stress in my life.

Journaling Pages for Statements 21 - 40

A lot of people say they want to get out of pain, but they aren't willing to make healing a high priority. They aren't willing to look inside to see the source of their pain in order to deal with it.

Lindsay Wagner

1. From the tapping statements between 1 - 20, list the top seven statements that you thought or felt applied to you:

1.

2.

3.

4.

5.

6.

7.

2. From this list of seven statements, select one and describe how it plays out in your life. Give an example or two. It is important to recognize and identify the pattern. Is there a trigger? How does it begin? How has it benefited you? How has it harmed you? For instance, do you have a fear of intimacy and the addiction gives you a place to hide, to be undesirable, thus unable to be in a significant-other, intimate relationship?

3. Tap out the top 7 statements.

4. As you were tapping out the statements, did you have any flashback or memories of the past, any additional insights, and/or ah-ha thoughts? If so, write them down. Make note of them.

41 – 60 EFT Tapping Statements

The trouble with life is, you are half way through it before you realize it's a 'do it yourself' thing.

Annie Zadra

41. I felt dead inside as a child.
42. I don't deserve to be loved.
43. My sadness drags me down.
44. I am limited in what I can do.
45. My needs are not important.
46. I am afraid of being rejected.
47. I am not lovable the way I am.
48. I am full of self-condemnation.
49. I am afraid of being found out.
50. I have no inner sense of worth.
51. I have an addictive personality.
52. My identity is that of an addict.
53. I feel hurt, depressed, and sad.
54. I feel lost and unsure of myself.
55. Nothing I do changes anything.
56. I feel lost, confused, and afraid.
57. I feel empty, lonely, and in pain.
58. I gave up hope a long time ago.
59. I am a failure at everything I do.
60. I am defective, damaged goods.

Journaling Pages for Statements 41 - 60

First we form habits, then they form us. Conquer your bad habits or they will conquer you.

Rob Gilbert

1. From the tapping statements between 1 - 20, list the top seven statements that you thought or felt applied to you:

1.

2.

3.

4.

5.

6.

7.

2. From this list of seven statements, select one and describe how it plays out in your life. Give an example or two. It is important to recognize and identify the pattern. Is there a trigger? How does it begin? How has it benefited you? How has it harmed you? For instance, have you learned how to handle everyday stresses? Or is it easier to reach for your addictive substance rather than manage your stress?

3. Tap out the top 7 statements.

4. As you were tapping out the statements, did you have any flashback or memories of the past, any additional insights, and/or ah-ha thoughts? If so, write them down. Make note of them.

61 – 80 EFT Tapping Statements

The capacity for hope is the most significant fact of life. It provides human beings with a sense of destination and the energy to get started.

Norman Cousins

61. Fulfilling my goals will not satisfy me.
62. There is something missing in my life.
63. I don't want to let go of my addiction.
64. I am self-righteous and self-centered.
65. My addiction is more powerful than me.
66. I am afraid to face life and my problems.
67. I feel guilty if I take any time just for me.
68. My needs were not important as a child.
69. I am incomplete and inadequate as I am.
70. I cannot be happy without my addiction.
71. I felt lost and unsure of myself as a child.
72. I am controlled by my drive for pleasure.
73. I am not satisfied or approving of myself.
74. I am alone and unprotected in the world.
75. I felt different from my friends as a child.
76. Nothing I do is right, good, or successful.
77. I am incomplete, weak, and incompetent.
78. The emptiness I feel inside is unbearable.
79. Nothing can be done about my addiction.
80. I have a hard time identifying my feelings.

Journaling Pages for Statements 61 - 80

The fear associated with venturing into the unknown is perfectly normal and to be expected. While it is normal to feel a certain amount of fear and apprehension when making changes, it is destructive to allow this fear to immobilize us, causing us to remain stuck in the status quo. We can instead use the fear and transform it into motivation to take positive action.

Jim Donovan

1. From the tapping statements between 1 - 20, list the top seven statements that you thought or felt applied to you:

1.

2.

3.

4.

5.

6.

7.

2. From this list of seven statements, select one and describe how it plays out in your life. Give an example or two. It is important to recognize and identify the pattern. Is there a trigger? How does it begin? How has it benefited you? How has it harmed you? For instance, do you have a fear of living your life, of being deserving and worthy? If so, do you focus on feelings of inadequacy and incompetence or feelings of being capable and powerful?

3. Tap out the top 7 statements.

4. As you were tapping out the statements, did you have any flashback or memories of the past, any additional insights, and/or ah-ha thoughts? If so, write them down. Make note of them.

81 – 100 EFT Tapping Statements

People who drink to drown their sorrow should
be told that sorrow knows how to swim.

Ann Landers

81. I will never have the things I want.
82. I am not comfortable in the world.
83. My addiction drains all my energy.
84. I feel unsafe and unsure of myself.
85. I am numb to my emotional needs.
86. I feel isolated, rejected, and alone.
87. I have hit bottom and can't get up.
88. No one knows about my addiction.
89. I cannot let others really know me.
90. I don't ask for what I need or want.
91. I hide my addiction from everyone.
92. I am defective, broken, and flawed.
93. I will be rejected when I am myself.
94. I know I will never amount to much.
95. I use my addiction to hide from life.
96. I am not whole or complete as I am.
97. I attack anything that threatens me.
98. I endure my life rather than enjoy it.
99. I am full of self-doubt and confusion.
100. I am powerless against my addiction.

Journaling Pages for Statements 81 – 100

We all fall into patterns and ruts. It takes courage, confidence, and guts to jump out of the ruts.

Unknown

1. From the tapping statements between 1 – 20, list the top seven statements that you thought or felt applied to you:

1.

2.

3.

4.

5.

6.

7.

2. From this list of seven statements, select one and describe how it plays out in your life. Give an example or two. It is important to recognize and identify the pattern. Is there a trigger? How does it begin? How has it benefited you? How has it harmed you? For instance, do you build walls so others will not see the imperfect you, so you won't be rejected, and you don't have to face your fears of getting close to someone? Do you feel worthy of a significant-other relationship?

3. Tap out the top 7 statements.

4. As you were tapping out the statements, did you have any flashback or memories of the past, any additional insights, and/or ah-ha thoughts? If so, write them down. Make note of them.

101 – 120 EFT Tapping Statements

The first and greatest form of courage is the courage to take responsible for your own life. Like it or not, you alone are responsible for the person you are today, the state of your heart, and the shape of your life. You can point your finger 'til the cows come home, but at the end of the day, the buck stops with you.

Margie Warrell

101. I hold onto my fear instead of releasing it.
102. I withdraw and isolate myself from others.
103. I don't know how to love and/or be loved.
104. I need my addictions to numb my feelings.
105. I know I am addicted to my addiction but...
106. The only thing I care about is getting high.
107. I don't know how to let go of my addiction.
108. I don't know how to open my heart to love.
109. I don't know how to heal my shattered self.
110. There is a void in me that my addiction fills.
111. I put other people's needs and desires first.
112. I wouldn't be an addict if my life was better.
113. I am ashamed of and hate my addictive self.
114. I felt unsafe and unsure of myself as a child.
115. I don't know who I am without my addiction.
116. Addictive highs are powerful and attractive.
117. I build walls and defenses to protect myself.
118. It is hard for me to be close to other people.
119. I am powerless to live my life any differently.
120. I watch TV and surf the internet to zone out.

Journaling Pages for Statements 101 - 120

You cannot make footprints in the sands of time if you are sitting on your butt and who wants to make butt prints in the sand of time?

Bob Moawad

1. From the tapping statements between 1 - 20, list the top seven statements that you thought or felt applied to you:

1.

2.

3.

4.

5.

6.

7.

2. From this list of seven statements, select one and describe how it plays out in your life. Give an example or two. It is important to recognize and identify the pattern. Is there a trigger? How does it begin? How has it benefited you? How has it harmed you? For instance, did you stop growing a long time ago? Is this because you don't know what you want to do with your life? Would you rather someone else to take care of you? Or could it be you are so apathetic about your life and there isn't any reason to grow?

3. Tap out the top 7 statements.

4. As you were tapping out the statements, did you have any flashback or memories of the past, any additional insights, and/or ah-ha thoughts? If so, write them down. Make note of them.

121 – 140 EFT Tapping Statements

As difficult as it seems, you can be sure of this: At the core of the heart, you have the power to move beyond the old issues that are still hindering your freedom. The hardest things, the ones that push you up against your limits, are the very things you need to address to make a quantum leap into a fresh inner and outer life.

Doc Childre and Howard Martin

121. I am insignificant, unworthy, and undeserving.
122. I don't know what joy, love, or peace feels like.
123. My addictive high numbs my pain and distress.
124. I don't know how to move forward with my life.
125. I don't know how to be safe in an unsafe world.
126. I will do anything to numb the pain I feel inside.
127. I am full of shame and guilt about my addiction.
128. I don't have the tools and skills to be successful.
129. It is not okay/safe for me to give up my addiction.
130. I am not willing to do anything about my addiction.
131. I didn't feel protected, loved, or nurtured as a child.
132. I reach for my addictive substance when I am lonely.
133. My addictive high gives me a feeling of completeness.
134. I reach for my addictive substance when I am stressed.
135. My primary relationship is with my addictive substance.
136. All I feel and know is shame, guilt, apathy, fear, and/or anger.
137. I reach for my addictive substance when I am feeling insecure.
138. My emotional stability is dependent on my addictive substance.
139. I am powerless against my addictive behavior and/or substance.
140. I will never be successful, loved, prosperous, powerful, accepted, peaceful, joyful, and/or happy. (Choose the three you most relate to.)

Journaling Pages for Statements 121 – 140

Where did we ever get the crazy idea that in order to make children do better, first we have to make them feel worse? Think of the last time you felt humiliated or treated unfairly. Did you feel like cooperating or doing better?

Jane Nelson

1. From the tapping statements between 1 – 20, list the top seven statements that you thought or felt applied to you:

1.

2.

3.

4.

5.

6.

7.

2. From this list of seven statements, select one and describe how it plays out in your life. Give an example or two. It is important to recognize and identify the pattern. Is there a trigger? How does it begin? How has it benefited you? How has it harmed you? For instance, are you defective, damaged goods? Do you feel lonely, empty, and in pain? Is it easier to be in pain than to heal yourself? If you are damaged goods, do you think you are worth saving? If you are lonely, do you seek out others or does your damaged self image prevent you from joining in with others? How can you break the cycle you seem to be looped into?

3. Tap out the top 7 statements.

4. As you were tapping out the statements, did you have any flashback or memories of the past, any additional insights, and/or ah-ha thoughts? If so, write them down. Make note of them.

Books by Tessa Cason

All Things EFT Tapping Manual

* Why does EFT Tapping work for some and not for others?
* How do you personalize EFT Tapping to be most effective for you?
* What is the very first tapping statement you need to tap?

This manual provides instructions on how to heal our disappointments, regrets, and painful memories.

EFT Tapping information has instructions on what to do if a tapping statement does not clear, what to do if tapping doesn't work for you, and how to write your own tapping statements.

We must eliminate the dysfunctional beliefs if we want to make changes in our lives. EFT Tapping can do just that. EFT Tapping is a simple, yet very powerful tool to heal our beliefs, emotions, painful memories, and stories.

500 EFT Tapping Statements for Moving Out of Survival

Survival is stress on steroids. It's feeling anxious and not good enough. Survival may be the most important topic we can heal within ourselves. Survival is programmed into our DNA.

Ella returned home from the market with her three year old daughter to find a note from her husband that he did not want to be married any longer. Under the note were divorce papers, the number of the divorce attorney, and $500.

Wanting to be able to give her daughter a wonderful childhood, she had to figure out how to survive and thrive. This is her story and the tapping statements she tapped.

Dr. John Montgomery says, "All 'negative,' or distressing, emotions, like fear, disgust, or anxiety, can be thought of as 'survival-mode' emotions: they signal that our survival and well-being may be at risk."

80 EFT Tapping Statements for Change

If it is not okay or safe for our lives to change, every time our lives change, the body is subjected to a tremendous amount of stress.

After graduating from high school, Charlie's dad told Charlie he could continue to live at home, but he would be charged room and board. At 18, Charlie was now financially responsible for himself. He was able to find a job and moved out.

Within a year, circumstances forced Charlie to move back home. Day after day, Charlie rode the bus to work. After work, he rode the bus home. One day as Charlie was riding the bus to work, he noticed another regular rider, Dan, tapping his head.

Together Dan and Charlie began tapping. Find out the results of their tapping and the statements they tapped.

300 EFT Tapping Statements for Self-defeating Behaviors, Victim, Self-pity

Tom had lots of excuses and reasons for his lack of "results." His boss, Robert MacGregor, saw the potential Tom had and asked his longtime friend, Sam Anderson, a life coach, to work with Tom. Read Tom's story to understand how Tom was able to step into his potential.

Self defeating behaviors take us away from our goals, from what we want, leaving us feeling exhausted, disempowered, and defeated. Self defeating thoughts are the negative thoughts we have about ourselves and/or the world around us such as "I'm not good enough", "I have to be perfect to be accepted."

Most likely, you have tried to change the self-defeating and self sabotage behavior, yet here you are with the same patterns.

100 EFT Tapping Statements for Feeling Fulfilled

John wasn't sure what would fulfill him. He loved his job and didn't want to find a new career, but he wasn't feeling fulfilled in his life. With the help of his wife, John found what would be fulfilling.

Fulfillment is a simple formula, actually. It's the follow-through that might be the problem.

What would prevent you from being fulfilled? Do you know what the blocks might be, the reason you remain out of sync, unfulfilled? Is it about leaving your comfort zone or maybe it's that you allow your limitations to define your life?

It is possible to remove the blocks, heal the beliefs on the subconscious level, and move toward your desire for fulfillment. To do so, we need a powerful tool. One such tool is EFT Tapping, the Emotional Freedom Technique.

Being Extraordinary

100 EFT Tapping Statements™ for Being Extraordinary! Tessa Cason

100 EFT Tapping Statements for Being Extraordinary!

Accomplishing extraordinary performances, having incredible successes, or earning large sums of money does not equate to an extraordinary person. This book is about discovering your extraordinary character.

Extraordinary – Exceeding ordinary, beyond ordinary.

Extraordinary starts with the self, our character, depth, and strength of our being. It's being congruent, walking our talk. It is the love, compassion, and tenderness we show ourselves. It's the pure and highest essence of our being.

Rebecca was approaching a time in her life in which she was doing some soul searching and examining her life. She didn't feel extraordinary. In her late 50s, she felt she was just ordinary. She reached out to Tessa. The email exchanges are included in this book along with tapping statements.

400 EFT Tapping Statements for Being Empowered and Successful

Being empowered is not about brute strength or the height of our successes. It is the strength, substance, and character of our inner being. It is knowing that whatever life throws at us, we will prevail.

Ava has just started a business with her two very successful sisters. She wants the business with her sisters to succeed, yet, she doesn't feel empowered. She doesn't want to feel as if the business would fail because of her and is ready to do the emotional work so she matches her sisters' power and success.

Sophie, Ava's roommate and an EFT practitioner-in-training, works with Ava. With Sophie's help, Ava begins to feel empowered and that her business with her sisters will be a success.

300 EFT Tapping Statements for Healing the Self

We live in a complex world with multiple influences. At birth, it starts with our parents and soon afterwards, the influence of other family members (grandparents, siblings, etc.), TV shows, cartoon characters, commercials, and peers. As we get older, we have the influences of teachers, coaches, tutors, television and movie stars, pop stars, sports heroes, and so many other.

When Pete was offered a promotion at work and was not excited about something he had worked so hard to accomplish, he knew he needed to find some answers. He thought he was living his mother's version of his life. He didn't know what brought him joy.

With the help of EFT and an EFT Practitioner, Pete was able to discover his version of his life, what brought him joy, and how to live a fulfilling life.

EFT Tapping for Anxiety, Fear, Anger, Self Pity, Courage (1,000 Tapping Statements)

Anxiety is a combination of 4 things: Unidentified Anger, Hurt, Fear, and Self Pity. We expect error, rejection, humiliation, and actually start to anticipate it.

When we are not in present time, we are either in the past or the future. Anger is the past. Fear is the future. Fear could actually be anger that we failed in the past and most likely will fail again in the future.

It takes courage on our part to heal the anxiety, identify the hurt, and to give up the self-pity. To heal, to thrive, and flourish, we need to address not only the Anxiety, but also the fear, anger, self pity, and hurt.

Healing is not about managing symptoms. It's about alleviating the cause of the symptoms.

80 EFT Tapping Statements for Feeling Less Than and Anxiety

Rene was excited for the year long mentoring program she enrolled in. *How wonderful*, she thought, *to be surrounded with like-minded people.* Five months into the program, she abruptly dropped out. Find out how her feeling Less Than and her Anxiety sabotaged her personal growth.

Anxiety has four parts: unidentified anger, hurt, fear, and self-pity. Living in a state of fear, we want a guarantee that our decisions and choices will produce the results or outcomes that we want. Feeling less than is played out in a cycle of shame, hopelessness, and self-pity. We feel shame about who we are, that we have little value, and that we are not good enough.

Feeling "less than" spirals down into depression, survival, and self-sabotage.

240 EFT Tapping Statements for Fear

Two months before school ended, Lennie was downsized from as a high school music teacher. When he was unable to find another job, fear crept into his thoughts. What if he couldn't find a job in music again? He wasn't qualified to do anything different. He was scared that he would not be able to support his family and they would end up homeless. He could feel the fear as his stomach was in knots.

Fear is that sense of dread, knots in the stomach, chill that runs down our spine, and the inability to breathe. We all know it. Fight-Flight-Freeze.

Fear is a self-protection mechanism. It is an internal alarm system that alerts us to potential harm. When we are in present time, we have the courage, awareness, wisdom, discernment, and confidence to identify and handle that which could cause us harm.

80 EFT Tapping Statements for Anxiety and Worry

"I just can't do this anymore," said Frank to his wife Mary. "You worry about everything. When we got married, your anxiety was something you did every now and then. But now you are paranoid about everything. I leave for work and you act like you are never going to see me again."

Anxiety is a combination of 4 things: unidentified anger, hurt, fear, self-pity. We expect error, rejection, humiliation, and actually start to anticipate it. It is an internal response to a perceived threat to our well-being. We feel threatened by an abstract, unknown danger that could harm us in the future.

Worry is a mild form of anxiety. Worry is a tendency to mull over and over and over anxiety-provoking thoughts. Worry is thinking, in an obsessive way, about something that has happened or will happen. Going over something again and again and asking, "What will I do? What should I have done?"

Healing a Broken Heart

200 EFT Tapping Statements™
for Healing a Broken Heart
Tessa Cason

200 ET Tapping Statements for Healing a Broken Heart

She found someone who made her feel cherished, valued, and loved. Tall, dark, and handsome as well as aware, present and understanding. Matt was an awesome guy. He thought she, too, was someone special, intriguing, and awesome.

Matt was promoted at work which meant months away from home and thus, decided to end their relationship. Her best friend introduced her to EFT Tapping to heal her broken heart.

Time does not heal all. Healing the grief of a broken heart is not easy. Grief is more than sadness. Grief is a loss. Something of value is gone. Grief is an intense loss that breaks our hearts.

Over time, unhealed grief becomes anger, blame, resentment, and/or remorse. To heal a broken heart, we need to identify, acknowledge, and healed the dysfunctional beliefs. EFT Tapping can help.

400 EFT Tapping Statements for Dealing with Emotions

Did you see the movie Pleasantville with Tobey Maguire and Reese Witherspoon, two siblings who are trapped in a 1950s black and white TV show, set in a small midwest town where everything is seemingly perfect. David and Jennifer (Tobey and Reese) must pretend they are Bud and Mary Sue Parker, the son and daughter in the TV show.

Slowly, the town begins changing from black and white to color as the townspeople begin to experience emotions. Experiencing emotions is like adding color to a black and white movie. Color adds a depth, enjoyment, and pleasure to the movie. Emotions add depth, enjoyment, and pleasure to our lives.

Emotions add animation, richness, and warmth to our lives. They give our lives meaning and fullness. Without emotions, our lives would be as boring as watching a black and white movie.

80 EFT Tapping Statements for Abandonment

Feelings of abandonment can be triggered by the ending of a relationship as well as the death of an individual. Even though we may have an intellectual understanding of death, there is still a feeling of abandonment when someone we treasure dies. For a small child, they do not understand death. They may still expect the parent to return at any time.

Even though Kevin drove an expensive sports car he wasn't the playboy type. He wanted to settle down and start a family. Kevin felt Susan could be "the one." He wanted to talk to her about taking their relationship to the next level.

Before Kevin could talk to Susan, she ended the relationship because of his insecurities in their relationship. She felt it had to do with the abandonment of his mom when he was a child. This book gives you the exact statements that Kevin tapped to deal with his insecurities in relationships.

A Broken Heart: Abandonment, Anger, Depression, Grief, Emotional Healing

EFT Tapping Statements for A Broken Heart: Abandonment, Anger, Depression, Grief, Emotional Healing (1,000 Statements)

Time does not heal all. When our hearts have been shattered, we feel nothing will ever be the same again. We are flooded with emotions... anger, grief, depression...

Regardless of what led to the broken heart, maybe a death, divorce, or a breakup, the result is the same...a broken heart. To heal a broken heart is not only about healing the grief, but also the feelings of abandonment, anger, and depression.

Being abandoned is a verb. It is something that "happens to us." The result of being abandoned is anger, grief, and depression. Grief is the sadness we experience when we have lost something of value.

In order to heal, we need to resolve the anger, grief, abandonment, and depression that resulted from our hearts being fractured.

200 EFT Tapping Statements for Wealth

After graduating from high school, Amy looked for a job for a solid year unsuccessfully! She lacked the necessary experience and education. She felt like she was in a vicious cycle, going round and round and round. Finally, she was hired at a large chain store. For the last eight years, she has been shuffled, unhappily, between different departments.

As a birthday gift, her mom gave her a session with an EFT Practitioner to determine what she wanted to do with her life. Follow along with Amy on her journey to self-discovery.

What we manifest in our lives is a direct result of our beliefs. If we have a mentality of wealth and abundance, we will prosper and thrive.

Our beliefs determine the level of our wealth and abundance. To heal our dysfunctional beliefs, we need a powerful tool. EFT Tapping is one such tool.

EFT Tapping Statements for
Prosperity, Survival, Courage,
Personal Power, Success
Tessa Cason

EFT Tapping Statements for Prosperity, Survival, Courage, Personal Power, Success (1,000 Statements)

What we believe determines our prosperity. Our beliefs determine our thoughts and feelings which in turn determine our choices and decisions. Therefore, what we manifest in our lives is a direct result of our beliefs. If we are happy and joyful, we will see happiness in everything. If we are fearful, we will see fear around every corner. If we have a mentality of abundance, we will prosper.

It is difficult to be prosperous when we are stuck in survival. In survival, we feel disempowered to thrive. We can only survive. It takes Courage to step into our Personal Power and to Succeed. We need a powerful tool to heal our dysfunctional beliefs. EFT Tapping is one such tool.

In this book, there are 200 tapping statements for each of these 5 topics - Prosperity, Survival, Courage, Personal Power, and Success.

80 EFT Tapping Statements for Abundance, Wealth, Money

Abby just had her 46th birthday. She tried to celebrate but she didn't have anything to be happy about. Her parents had died in a car accident the Christmas before while driving home from her new home after celebrating Christmas. Both of her parents were real estate agents. She was their transaction coordinator. The three of them had their own offices, handling any real estate transaction that someone might need. Without them, she had no real estate transactions to coordinate.

Abby funds were running dry. She had applied for jobs without success. Abby talked to every one she and her parents knew in hopes of finding a job. With the slow real estate market, she was unable to find any work.

Find out how Abby turned her life around and the exact statements that Abby tapped to deal with her monetary issues.

400 EFT Tapping Statements™
for Dreams to Reality
Tessa Cason

400 EFT Tapping Statements for Dreams to Reality

Have you done everything you were supposed to do for your dreams to become reality? You were clear on what they were. You made your vision boards with lots of pictures of what you desired. You visualized them coming true and living that life. You've stated your affirmations over and over and over for their fulfillment. You released and allowed the Universe to handle the details. And, now, dust is collecting on your vision boards and you are still waiting for the Universe to handle the details.

Our dreams are our hopes and desires of what we want to come true one day. They are snapshots of what we want our future to be. Yet, sometimes, maybe most of the time, our dreams do not become reality and never manifest themselves in our lives. We gave up on our dreams a long time ago.

Jane shares her story of how she used EFT Tapping to turn her dreams into reality.

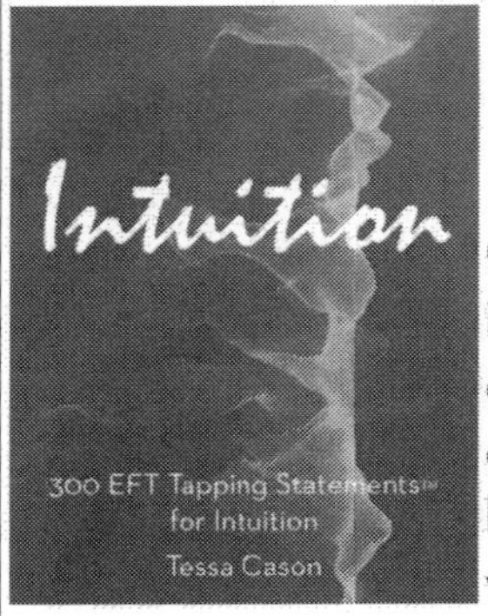

300 ET Tapping Statements for Intuition

Quinn was one of Tessa's students in her Developing Your Intuition class. She had been hesitant to develop her intuition. One of her basic needs was Belonging. If she was intuitive, she might not belong and thus, realized this was part of her hesitation.

She also had a tendency to avoid which also wasn't conductive to developing her intuition. Tessa wrote out some EFT Tapping statements for her to tap:
* I ignore my inner voice.
* No one I know uses intuition.
* I'm too logical to be intuitive.
* Being intuitive is too complicated.

Included in this book are exercises and helpful hints to develop your intuition as well info on Symbolism, Colors, Number, Charkas, Asking Questions of Our Intuition, Archetypes, and 36 Possible Reasons We Took Physical Form.

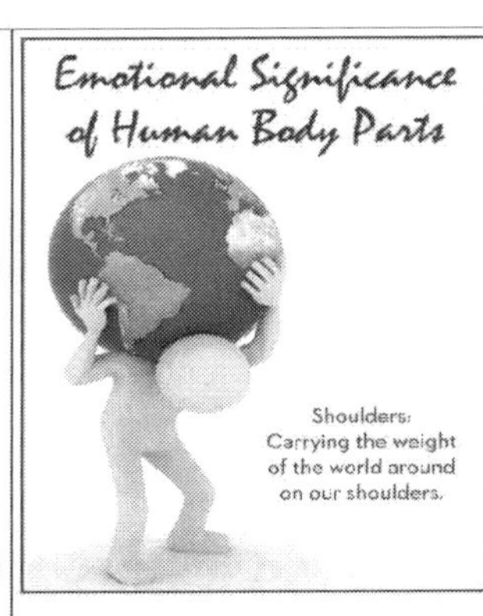

Emotional Significance of Human Body Parts.Chasing the Pain

"We carry the weight of the world around on our shoulders." The emotional significance of the shoulder is about responsibility

The body "talks" to us...in its language. To understand what the body is saying, we need to learn the body's language

Jona greeted me at the airport gate on crutches. After hugging each other, she asked what the left ankle meant. I told her the left side of the body had to do with what's going on in the inside and the ankles had to do with commitments.

She had been dating a man for the last two months and he just proposed.

Chasing the Pain is a technique with EFT Tapping tha as we tap for a physical pain we are experiencing, the original pain might disappear only to be felt in a different part of the body.

100 EFT Tapping Statements for Accepting Our Uniqueness and Being Different

Brian was an intelligent high school student with average grades. He tested high on all the assessment tests. Brian didn't think of himself as intelligent since his grades were only average. He didn't plan on going to college because he thought he wasn't smart enough and would flunk out.

His counselor knew otherwise and suggested Brian retake the tests to see if the tests were wrong. Find out Brian's scores after he retook the tests and how Mr. Cole introduced EFT Tapping to Brian.

If you were your unique self, do you fear being alone, rejected, or labeled as "undesirable?" Or maybe it's being laughed at and ridiculed for being different and unique?

When we play our lives safe, we end up feeling angry, anxious, powerless, hopeless, and depressed.

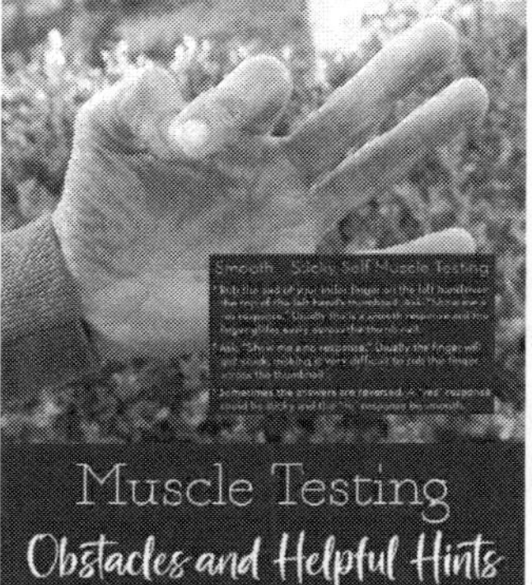

Muscle Testing.Obstacles and Helpful Hints

Muscle testing is a method in which we can converse with the subconscious mind as well as the body's nervous system and energy field.

This book details 10 obstacles and 10 helpful hints to successfully muscle test.

One obstacle is that it is a necessity that the tester be someone that calibrates the same, or above, that of the testee, on David Hawkins' Map of Consciousness or be in the higher altitudes, 250 or higher, on the Map.

Helpful hint: When muscle testing, the tester and testee should not make eye contact with each other. With eye contact, the answer would be "our" energy instead of the "testee's" energy.

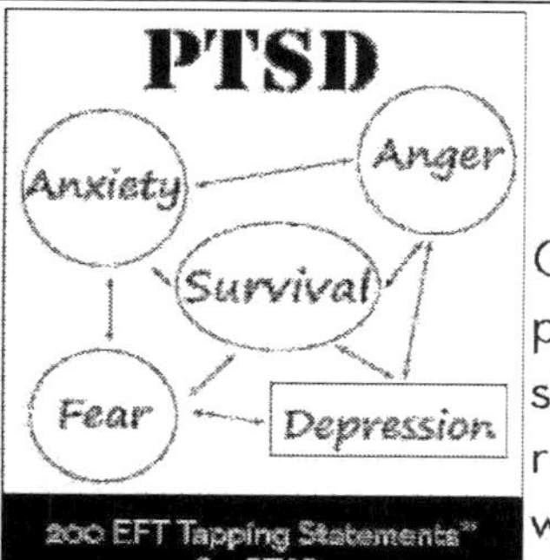

200 EFT Tapping Statements for PTSD

George believed that if he prepared for his death, it was signaling the Universe he was ready to die. George did die without preparing his wife.

George took care of everything. The only thing Helen had to take care of George.

After George died, she had no idea if they owned the home they lived in, if George had life insurance, how to pay bills, if they had money, if they did, where was it? She didn't know if George had left a will. She was not prepared for George's death or how to take care of everything that George took care of.

With the help of friends and EFT Tapping, Helen was able to heal and learn how to take care of everything that George once did.

Healing is not about managing symptoms. It is about alleviating the cause of the symptoms.

EFT Tapping Statements for PTSD, Survival, Disempowered, Fear, Anger (1,200 Statements)

The potential exists for anyone that is in any life threatening situation in which they fear for their life, that believes death is imminent, to experience PTSD.

With PTSD, our Survival is at stake. As a result of our survival being threatened, we feel Disempowered to thrive. We can only survive. When we are caught in Survival, Fear is a prevalent emotion. When we feel Disempowered, Anger is just beneath the surface.

To heal, to thrive, and flourish, we need to address not only the PTSD, but also Survival and Feeling Disempowered, Fear, and Anger. (Thus, the 5 topics in this PTSD Workbook.)

Healing PTSD is a process in which we must desensitize, decrease, and heal the survival response. EFT Tapping is the best method to do so.

200 EFT Tapping Statements for Conflict

"Hi, Julia. So glad you called." Excitedly, I said, "I just finished decorating the house and I'm ready for Christmas!"

Not at all thrilled to be talking to her sister-on-law, Julia said, "That's why I'm calling. You don't mind if I host the family Christmas get-together, do you?"

A little surprised, I said, "Well, I do.

"Tough," she said. "I'm hosting Christmas this year."

This wasn't the first "conflict" with her sister-in-law. But, Audrey was a conflict coward and did not engage.

After EFT Tapping, Audrey overcame her issues with conflict. Find out how and who hosted Christmas that year!

80 EFT Tapping Statements for Anger

Doug was immensely proud of his son, Andy, until he watched his son (a high school senior) jeopardize his chance at an athletic scholarship to attend college. The count was 3-2, three balls and two strikes. The final pitch was thrown and Andy let it go by. The umpire shouts, "Strike!" Andy has just struck out.

"What's wrong with your eyes old man?" Andy shouts at the umpire. "That was a ball. It wasn't in the strike zone. Need instant replay so you can see it in slow motion? I'm not out!"

Andy, was following his father's example of being a rageaholic. EFT Tapping helped both Doug and Andy to take control of his life and his anger.

Anger is not right or wrong, healthy or unhealthy. It is the expression of anger that makes it right or wrong, healthy or unhealthy.

400 ET Tapping Statements for Being a Champion

Jack was a professional runner that injured himself at the US Championships. He was unable to compete at the World Championship. The previous year, Jack had won gold at the World Championships. After six months, he still was not able to run even though the doctors assured him he should be able to run. He had exhausted all medical and physical therapy treatments without success or hope of being able to run pain-free.

Our of frustration, Jack decided to look at the mental piece with a transformation coach. Follow Jack's recovery back to the track through EFT Tapping.

Champions are rare. If being a champion was easy then everyone would be a champion and a champion would not be anything special. It is in the difficulty of the task that, once accomplished, makes a champion great.

EFT Tapping Statements for Champion, Personal Power, Success, Self Confidence, Role Model (1,000 Statements)

Being a champion is more than just being successful. It is the achievement of excellence. It is more than just being competent. It is about stepping into one's power. It is more than just setting goals. It is the achievement of those goals with perseverance, dedication, and determination. It is not just about the practicing, training, and learning. It is the application and implementation of the training and learning into a competition and into everyday situations.

Champions are successful, but not all successful people are champions. Champions are powerful, but not all powerful people are champions. Champions are confident but not all confident people are champions. Champions dream big but not all people that dream big are champions.

300 EFT Tapping Statements for Dealing with Obnoxious People

Three siblings were each dealing with an obnoxious person in their lives. Katherine was dealing with a co-worker that took credit for her accomplishments.

Megan, a professional athlete, was distracted by a narcissistic team member that disrupted practice and thus, her performances at meets.

Peter was a very successful college student that had a Teaching Assistant jealous of everything that Peter was and the TA was not.

Read how each resolved and solved their issue with an obnoxious person.

80 EFT Tapping Statements for Self Esteem

Ron had driven a semi-trailer truck for 30 years for the same company. To celebrate his 60th birthday and 30 years of service his company had a celebration for him. After the celebration, Ron's boss suggested that he find a job that was more age appropriate. Ron's lack of self-esteem was interfering with moving on with his life. This book gives you the exact statements that Ron tapped to heal his lack of self esteem, self respect, and self-pride.

From birth to about the age of seven, we learn self love from mom. From about the age of seven through twelve, from dad we learn self esteem, earned loved. Self esteem is about the feelings, respect, and pride we have in ourselves.

The lack of self esteem shows up in our lives as a lack self respect and/or pride in ourselves. This "lack" will taint every area of our lives.

340 ET Tapping Statements for Healing From the Loss of a Loved One

Grief is more than sadness. It is more than unhappiness. Grief is a loss. Something of value is gone. Grief is an intense loss that breaks our heart. Loss can be the death of a loved one, a pet, a way of life, a job, a marriage, one's own imminent death. Grief is real.

Over time, unhealed grief becomes anger, resentment, blame, and/or remorse. We become someone that we are not. It takes courage to move through the grief and all the emotions buried deep within.

John's father died of a heart attack while gardening. A year after his death, John still was not able to move on or be happy. His wife handed him a business card of an EFT Practitioner and recommended therapy to heal the grief. After working with the Practitioner, John was able to find his joy again.

100 EFT Tapping Statements for Feeling Deserving

Sarah, a sophomore in college, was unsure of what to declare as her major. She met with a guidance counselor who wanted to chat first.

Sarah thought of herself as an accident since she had two older siblings who had already moved out of the house when she was five. Her parents had been looking forward to an empty nest, instead, they had a third child that was just starting school.

Sarah had felt undeserving her whole life, even though her parents loved her dearly and never treated her life an accident.

Travel the path Sarah walked with the counselor to finally feel deserving.

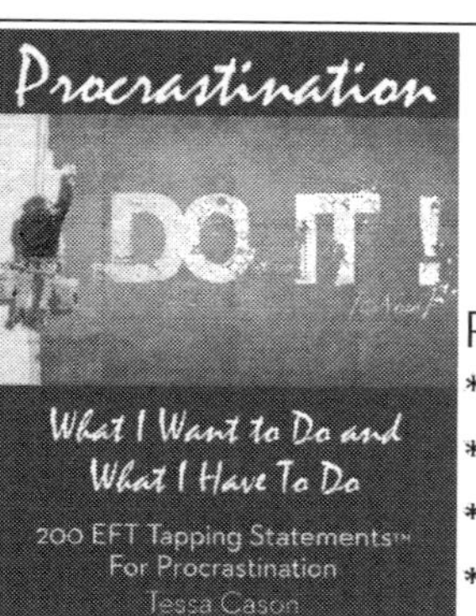

200 EFT Tapping Statements for Procrastination.What I Want to Do and What I Have to Do

Procrastination is about avoiding.
* What are we avoiding?
* What are we afraid to find out?
* What are we not wanting to do?
* What are we not willing to face?

Is it:
* We don't have the tools and skills to do something.
* Rebellion
* Lack of motivation.
* Not knowing what needs to be done.
* Poor time management.

The list is long why we procrastinate and what it could be about. What do we do to heal our procrastination tendencies? EFT Tapping. To heal we have to be able to recognize, acknowledge, and take ownership of that which we want to heal. Then we have to delete the dysfunctional beliefs on the subconscious level. EFT is one such tool that can do just that.

I Love Me!

80 EFT Tapping Statements™ for Relationship with Self
Tessa Cason

80 EFT Tapping Statements for Relationship with Self

Stephanie, now 55 years old, used to be excited about life and about her life. That was 35 years ago. She was engaged to the love of her life. A month before the wedding her fiancée ran off with a beauty queen.

After 35 years, Stephanie still felt defeated, beaten, defective, broken, and flawed. She was still resentful. She had become comfortable in apathy because she did not know how to move beyond her self-pity.

With the help of EFT Tapping, Stephanie was able to heal her wounded self and begin to live life again.

Do you feel disconnected from yourself? Do you feel as if you could never be whole? Do you feel defeated by life? To change our lives, we have to be able to recognize, acknowledge, and take ownership of that which we want to change. Then heal the dysfunctional beliefs on a subconscious level. EFT Tapping can help.

700 ET Tapping Statements for Weight, Emotional Eating, & Food Cravings

Emma's sister's wedding was fast approaching. She would be asked at the wedding how her diet was going.

Emma has struggled with her weight for the last 35 years, since high school. Out of desperation, Hannah began working with an EFT Practitioner. Follow her journey to healing the cause of her weight issues.

Excess weight, food cravings, emotional eating, and overeating are symptoms of deeper unresolved issues beneath the weight. Attempting to solve the problem by only dealing with the symptoms is ineffective and does not heal the issue.

Weight is the symptom. The usual programs for weight loss aren't working because they are attempting to solve the problem by dealing with the symptom instead of healing the cause.

EFT Tapping Statements for Weight + Food Cravings, Anger, Grief, Not Good Enough, Failure (1,150 Statements)

Excess weight, food cravings, emotional eating, and overeating are symptoms of deeper issues beneath the weight. Attempting to solve the problem by only dealing with the symptoms is ineffective and does not heal the issue.

The usual programs for weight loss aren't working because they are attempting to solve the problem by dealing with the symptom instead of healing the cause.

IF WE WANT TO HEAL OUR WEIGHT ISSUES, WE NEED TO HEAL THE CAUSE...THE DYSFUNCTIONAL BELIEFS AND EMOTIONS.

HEALING IS NOT ABOUT MANAGING SYMPTOMS. IT'S ABOUT ALLEVIATING THE CAUSE OF THE SYMPTOMS.

80 EFT Tapping Statements for Addictions

Derrick's mom died when he was a senior in high school. His dad (an alcoholic) told Derrick that as soon as he graduated from high school, he was on his own.

The day that Derrick graduated from high school, he went down and enlisted in the army. In the army, he started to drink. A month after his enlistment concluded, he met a wonderful woman. They married and had a child.

One day when Derrick returned home from the bar, he found an empty house and a note. The note told him that since has unwilling to admit he was an alcoholic or to go to counseling, she was left with only one choice. That choice was to relocate herself and their daughter to some place safe, away from him.

Derrick felt he had nothing to live for. He discovered someone at work that was a recovering alcoholic. She introduced her secret, EFT Tapping, to Derrick.

80 EFT Tapping Statements for Weight and Emotional Eating

Excess weight is a symptom, not the cause of overeating and emotional eating.

The day that Tracy was graduating from UCLA, she received a phone call that her father had fallen and had been hospitalized. She was on the next flight home to Dallas. It was decided that her father needed surgery and that Tracy should stay on for a short while to care for her dad. No one asked Tracy what she wanted. But, she stayed anyway.

Seven months later, even though her father had mended, Tracy had become her father's caregiver. This is not what Tracy had planned to do with her life after graduating from college. Every month, over the course of the seven unhappy months, Tracy's weight spiraled up, until she was at her highest weight EVER.

This book gives you the exact statements that Tracy tapped to heal the cause of her weight gain.

80 ET Tapping Statements for Manifesting a Romantic Relationship

Tanya tells the story about her best friend, Nica. Nica wants a relationship. She wants to be in love, the happily-ever-after kind of love. Nica is self-absorbed, self-centered, smart, and pretty.

Nica has had several long-term relationships but, never allows anyone close enough to get to know her. When she is in between boyfriends, she always whines:

* No man will ever want me.
* The odds are slim to none that I will find anyone.
* I have a bad track record with men so I give up.
* There will never be anyone for me.
* My desires will never be fulfilled.

Tanya is a tapper and finally Nica agrees to do some tapping as a last resort! The Tapping Statements that Nica tapped to manifest a relationship are listed in this eBook.

80 EFT Tapping Statements for Social Anxiety

In social settings, Johnny felt very awkward. He did not enjoy the limelight or any attention focused on him at all!

"Dude," Johnny's buddies would say. "When are you going to get over this fear of talking to a woman?" Johnny would laugh off their comments.

Social Anxiety - Dreading, fearing, and/or expecting to be rejected and/or humiliated by others in social settings.

* A feeling of discomfort, fear, dread, or worry that is centered on our interactions with other people.
* Fear of being judged negatively by others.
* Fear of being evaluated negatively by others.

Is there hope for those that have social anxiety? Yes. EFT Tapping. Tap the statements that Johnny tapped to overcome his social anxiety.

80 EFT Tapping Statements for Adult Children of Alcoholics

Did you have a parent that was an alcoholic? Do you have difficulty relating and connecting to others? Do you have a strong need to be perfect? Is your self-esteem low and judge yourself harshly? Do you have a fear of abandonment and rejection? If so, then EFT Tapping might help.

Rebecca had lost her 4th job. She was defensive, argumentative, and resentful. Rebecca knew her boss was right in firing her.

Rebecca's childhood was anything but idyllic. Her father was a raging alcoholic. She was terrified of his anger. Rebecca tried to be perfect so her dad couldn't find fault with her. Home life was hell. She had to grow up really fast and was never allow to be a kid or to play.

Rebecca did see an EFT Practitioner and was able to heal the anger, the need to be perfect, and other issues one has when they have an alcoholic parent.

200 EFT Tapping Statements for Knowing God

So many questions surround this topic, God. Does God exist or is God a fabrication? Is God for real or just a concept? If God does exist, then what is God's role in our lives?

Do our prayers get answered or are we praying in vain? Does God make mistakes? God created Lucifer and then kicked out a third of his angels from heaven along with Lucifer. Was Lucifer a mistake and all the angels that choose to follow Lucifer? Do we just want to believe that a supreme being really cares about us, gave us our lives' purpose, a mission, and a destiny? God is as varied as there are people.

Many have said that God gave humans the power of choice and free will. If this is true, the consequences of our actions are ours alone. Yet, there are those who believe that God could intervene. God should take action to protect and provide for us.

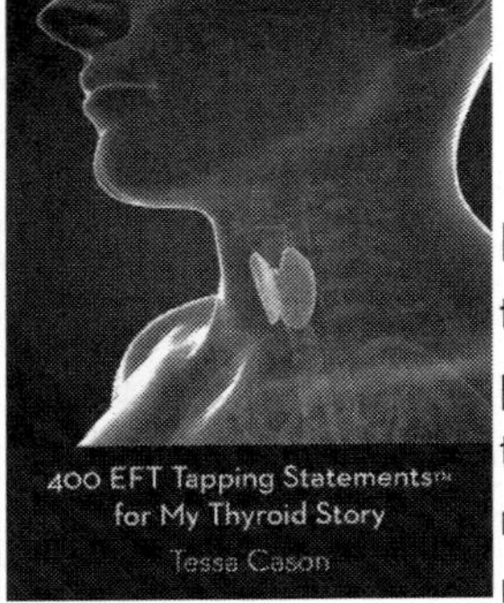

400 ET Tapping Statements for My Thyroid Story

In 2005, I was diagnosed with thyroid cancer. I researched the potential cause and discovered that 20 years after exposure to natural gas, thyroid issues will result. 20 years previous to the diagnosis, I lived in a townhouse for 850 days that had a gas leak.

While pursuing healing modalities after the exposure to natural gas, I began to realize that about 50% of our health issues are emotionally produced. The other 50% are the result of environmental factors such as smoking, chemicals, accidents, and/or hereditary.

I did not believe my emotional issues caused the thyroid cancer. It was the result of an environmental factor outside myself. BUT, since the thyroid was affected, if I worked on the emotional issues that had to do with the thyroid, it should impact the thyroid cancer. That was my theory.

100 EFT Tapping Statements for Fear of Computers

Can you image strapping on your Jet pack to get to work? Traveling on the Hyperloop that travels at speeds up to 600 mph to visit a friend that lives in another state? Stepping into your self-driving car that chauffeurs you to the restaurant? Soon all of these will be a part of our lives.

Modern technology! Most everyone knows that the computer can answer most any question. Most every job today and jobs of the future require at least some knowledge of computers.

Grandmere was intimidated by the computer. Her motivation was her granddaughter would was moving to another country. Granddaughter wants her to learn to use the computer so they can Skype when she is out of the country. Read how Grandmere was able to overcome her anxiety and fear of the computer.

200 EFT Tapping Statements for Sex

Is sex about the act or is sex about the intimacy shared by the act? Is sex about the orgasms or is it about the connection, touching, and cuddling?

In most culture, sex/lovemaking/intercourse is not discussed, explored, or a polite topic of conversation. For a fulfilling and satisfying sexual relationship, communication is important, yet many couples find it difficult to talk about sex.

Can you talk to your partner about sex?
Are you comfortable with your sexuality?
Do you know your partner's sexual strategy?

Our attitude, beliefs, and emotions determine our thoughts and feeling about sex. Dysfunctional beliefs can interfere with a healthy, fulfilling, satisfying sexual relationship. If we want to make changes in our lives, we have to recognize, acknowledge, and take ownership of our dysfunctional beliefs and emotions.

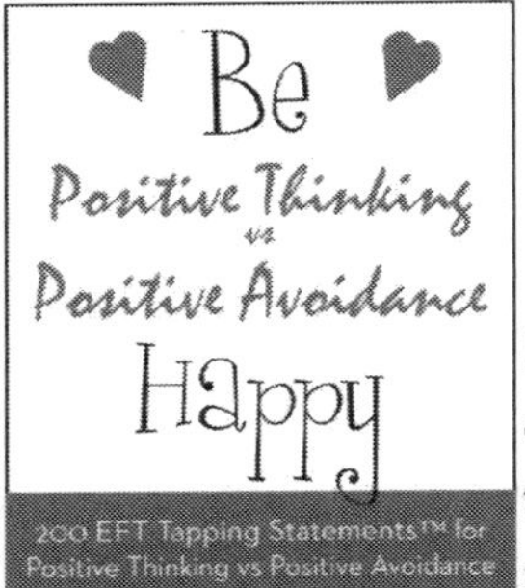

200 EFT Tapping Statements for Positive Thinking vs Positive Avoidance

If we keep piling more Band-Aids over a wound, the wound is still there. At some point, the wound needs to be examined, cleaned, and treated in order for heal.

Sometimes it is just "easier" to think positive when we really don't want to look at an issue. Positive Avoidance is denying the truth of a situation. It is a denial of our experience and our feelings about the situation.

When we try to push down our negative emotions, it is like trying to push a ball underwater. The ball pops back up.

Positive Thinking is the act of thinking good or affirmative thoughts, finding the silver lining around a dark cloud, and looking on the more favorable side of an event or condition. It is not denial, avoidance, or false optimism.

Books and Kindles eBooks by Tessa Cason

80 EFT Tapping Statements for:
Abandonment
Abundance, Wealth, Money
Addictions
Adult Children of Alcoholics
Anger and Frustration
Anxiety and Worry
Change
"Less Than" and Anxiety
Manifesting a Romantic Relationship
Relationship with Self
Self Esteem
Social Anxiety
Weight and Emotional Eating

100 EFT Tapping Statements for Accepting Our Uniqueness and Being Different
100 EFT Tapping Statements for Being Extraordinary!
100 EFT Tapping Statements for Fear of Computers
100 EFT Tapping Statements for Feeling Deserving
100 EFT Tapping Statements for Feeling Fulfilled
200 EFT Tapping Statements for Conflict
200 EFT Tapping Statements for Healing a Broken Heart
200 EFT Tapping Statements for Knowing God
200 EFT Tapping Statements for Positive Thinking vs Positive Avoidance
200 EFT Tapping Statements for Procrastination
200 EFT Tapping Statements for PTSD
200 EFT Tapping Statements for Sex
200 EFT Tapping Statements for Wealth
240 EFT Tapping Statements for Fear
300 EFT Tapping Statements for Healing the Self
300 EFT Tapping Statements for Dealing with Obnoxious People
300 EFT Tapping Statements for Intuition
300 EFT Tapping Statements for Self-defeating Behaviors, Victim, Self-pity
340 EFT Tapping Statements for Healing From the Loss of a Loved One
400 EFT Tapping Statements for Being a Champion
400 EFT Tapping Statements for Being Empowered and Successful
400 EFT Tapping Statements for Dealing with Emotions
400 EFT Tapping Statements for Dreams to Reality
400 EFT Tapping Statements for My Thyroid Story

500 EFT Tapping Statements for Moving Out of Survival
700 EFT Tapping Statements for Weight, Emotional Eating, and Food Cravings
All Things EFT Tapping Manual
Emotional Significance of Human Body Parts
Muscle Testing - Obstacles and Helpful Hints

EFT Tapping Statements for:

A Broken Heart, Abandonment, Anger, Depression, Grief, Emotional Healing
Anxiety, Fear, Anger, Self Pity, Change
Champion, Success, Personal Power, Self Confidence, Leader/Role Model
Prosperity, Survival, Courage, Personal Power, Success
PTSD, Disempowered, Survival, Fear, Anger
Weight & Food Cravings, Anger, Grief, Not Good Enough, Failure

Other Books

Why we Crave What We Crave: The Archetypes of Food Cravings
How to Heal Our Food Cravings

EFT Workbook and Journal for Everyone:

Abandonment
Abundance, Money, Prosperity
Addictions
Adult Children of Alcoholics
Anger, Apathy, Guilt
Anxiety/Worry
Being A Man
Being, Doing, Belonging
Champion
Change
Conflict
Courage
Dark Forces
Decision Making
Depression
Difficult/Toxic Parents
Difficult/Toxic People
Emotional Healing

Fear
Forgiveness
God
Grief
Happiness/Joy
Intuition
Leadership
Live Your Dreams
Life Purpose/Mission
People Pleaser
Perfectionism
Personal Power
Relationship w/Others
Relationship w/Self & Commitment to Self
Self Confidence
Self Worth/Esteem
Sex
Shame
Stress
Success
Survival
Transitions
Trust/Discernment
Victim, Self-pity, Self-Defeating Behavior, Shadow Self
Weight and Emotional Eating

Made in the USA
Middletown, DE
26 October 2022

13542705R00040